a good death

a good death

John Anthony Noonan

Compiled and edited
by Karen Noonan

Buffalo Arts Publishing

◀◥P Buffalo Arts Publishing

Email: info@buffaloartspublishing.com

*Front cover design by John Noonan from a photograph of
Christopher Clements (p. 120)*

Publisher's Cataloging-in-Publication data

Noonan, John Anthony.
  A Good death / John Anthony Noonan ; compiled and edited by
  Karen Noonan.
  pages cm
  ISBN 978-0-6924-6782-4

1. Clements, Christopher. 2. Noonan, John Anthony. 3. AIDS (Disease)
--Patients --Biography. 4. AIDS (Disease) --Patients --United States –
Death. 5. Buffalo (N.Y.) --Social life and customs. 6. Gay couples. 7.
Gay men --Biography. I. Noonan, Karen. II. Title.

RC607.A26 N64 2015
362.1/969792/0092 –dc23   2015950804

for those behind a wheelchair

CONTENTS

John Noonan and Christopher Clements

FOREWORD

John Noonan died suddenly in 2007. It seems fitting that he did not have to suffer from a long illness after having cared for his partner, Christopher Clements, through his six-year battle with AIDS. It had been eight years since Chris's death, but Chris and "the good death" were never far from John's thoughts. He was never satisfied with his work, and there were multiple versions of most chapters of this book. The preface is incomplete, but according to his notes he wanted the reader to know "how I got here". What I have compiled here is the most complete version gleaned from his numerous writings and notes.

John was a gifted musician, songwriter, and artist. He started writing prose only when he decided to write this book, but he had always been an inspired storyteller. In his youth, he was an actor and appeared off Broadway in "40 Deuce" and "Great Expectations". At age sixteen, he had left high school after being "outed" at a school assembly and went to London, where he knew no one, and quickly became, as the story went, a glitter-greeter at a happening nightclub.

After moving to New York City, he had many different jobs. He was a chef, a bartender, a club/restaurant manager, and a designer and renovator. He had told his father when he left school that he could never work a nine to five job, and he never did.

John's greatest passion was music, and he took refuge in his music during Chris's illness. Somehow, he found time to work on recording his music and rehearsing with his singer, Sandy Bell, until the last year of Chris's illness. Sadly, he never pursued getting his music out to the public. He admitted having a fear of success, which was surprising because he was so brave.

The care and patience John gave Chris during his ten-year battle with AIDS was inspirational to all of us who knew them. John was well known for being oblivious to time. When you were with him, he gave you his full attention. He took a heartfelt interest in all his family members and friends, and we were all fortunate to have him in our lives.

Foreword

To watch Chris deteriorate was heart-breaking. His zest for life had been remarkable. When John and Chris would arrive for our family vacation with their cat, TeaBag, they had barely unpacked before Chris had on his roller blades and was ready to risk the narrow streets, despite John's protests. He said his mind was like flypaper – everything stuck to it – and we would fight over being on his Trivial Pursuit team. The stories he told of his youthful adventures growing up in the south were fantastic. My favorite was the time he put soap into the fountain in the town square and caused a bubble flood. Even when he could barely walk with the help of his walker, he still went in the ocean and floated around a bit. He didn't give up easily.

People said Chris was lucky to have John – and he was – but John was lucky to have Chris as well. They shared a sense of humor and a good life. Together they defeated alcoholism, beat lymphoma, battled AIDS, and ultimately achieved "a good death".

Karen Noonan

PREFACE

Monday, April 2006

The phone rang on a Monday around dinnertime. It was Karen, my brother Fran's wife and my close friend, calling from Buffalo, my hometown.

"Hi John," she said in clear 'prepare yourself' dark elongated tones. "Well ... Fran and I just got back from Mom and Dad's, and ... Mom looks really bad. Even Fran said so, and he never has said it before. She's really out of it. I think she may be going. Sorry ..."

"Do you think I should come now?"

"Well ... yes."

The next afternoon I arrived at my parents' house, hugged my father, and went directly to their blue bedroom. She was in a twin hospital bed parked alongside the double bed they had shared since long before I was born. I spent all my young sicknesses on that remarkable thing. We all did, all eight of us Noonan children. It was her way of making you feel special when you felt less than privileged to be barfing or sweating a fever – or a leaky worse.

We weren't kids who crawled in bed with the folks on a weekend morning. We all wore full pajamas – all the time – and their bed was theirs. One might transgress on a sibling's territory – but not Mom and Dad's blue master bedroom – at night or in the morning, when they would emerge fully dressed and ready to "rouse the troops", as my father fondly called it.

"Yoo hoo! Rise and shine!" was my mother's version. Along with opening your shades and windows. "La dee dum" or "Oooh, my! What a beautiful day!" I kid you not. This would seem intolerable except she really felt that way.

Now, the shock of bright light accompanied by enough sugar to put you in diabetic shock first thing in the morning sounds unforgivable (especially during the drug addled teen years). It wasn't a show. She'd go off down the hallway "la dee dahing" or "bum ba dumming". She loved fresh air, birdies, babies, strangers, snow, flowers, or whatever nature offered that day.

She didn't "care for" disciplining, laziness, "vulgar" names, "letting yourself go", or pain. I learned this as she battled bouts with hypothyroidism and what seemed to be colitis. I often likened her health scenario to that of a bird. She was flying free – as long as she didn't get her wings wet.

She kept reams of journals on our health and, in later years, hers. A real note taker, she was also a big note maker. We had a note taped over the kitchen sink for what seemed years that said, "Shut Your Mouth!" This was to encourage breathing through your nose – and hence not swallowing air and causing bloating. It also gave her the last word on all the "SHUT UPS" she was stuck hearing us blurt all day. This phrase was "Bold" or "Vulgar", especially delivered by your red-faced brat or world wary teenager.

"If you don't have anything nice to say – don't say anything at all." Each time she said this like it was a new idea.

When the thyroid problem seemed to plague her very soul, "MUSIC! MUSIC! MUSIC!" She would enter and play Rachmaninoff REAL LOUD. I grew up with her romantic period piano music permeating the score of my early years.

a good death

And here she lay in the late afternoon sun, jaws open, heaving for breath, with her tender eye lids barely closed. Each breath was a Herculean struggle, so how she could be sleeping was a mystery. I watched her for around a half hour, then I crawled on to my old sick spot on the big bed, next to her railed rental, and she popped her eyes wide and focused. "OH, JOHHN," raising her arms. I was on all fours, leaned in to kiss her on either cheek (the European way she liked), and let her hold my face for the few seconds she could, like it was the world's biggest diamond.

Me: Your Black Sheep is here.
Her: NO (gasp) BLACK

Preface

Me: Sorry I didn't bring you anything.
Her: Your LOVE!
I laid back, my head by her feet.
Me: Now, Mom, just because you're not feeling 100% is no reason to let yourself go.

NO RESPONSE. She had returned to the process of heaving for each breath with intense determination. She'd been struggling for each breath for almost a week – where was this stamina from? She'd been frail for a few years now – and at 87? Having asthma, I could only begin to imagine how intensely her ribs ached.

My stunned father sat in the living room looking out the window. "It's hard to believe it was just a week ago we were walking out there. She told me on Sunday she wouldn't be here long." (pause) "I thought I'd have her at least another year."

He was what I call "turning the car around". A five point turn on a road you don't want to be on that forms a star in space, a most beautiful one made of reluctant charity and acceptance of the unthinkable and sparkling with the selflessness that is the true love that only my father has for my mother.

That's Not What I Mean

Saturday morning, April 3,1999. Home.

I don't recall waking up, but I did. As was my routine at this point, I'd look at his face, roll out of bed, and check the bed pads, then the morphine/saline drip bags and lines. Then I'd go make coffee, light a cigarette, visit the bathroom to splash, brush, and make a splash.

Then my well worn...

Me: Good morning sugar.

This was done with delicate pets, a loving hand rotating in an available spot that could stimulate waking. His eyes opened instantly in that wide-eyed yet detached intensity. What incredible focus he had now. As if he hadn't been sleeping at all. I saw his customary eyeball scan to check – down the bed, to his needled hand, and then up into my eyes. Only after all this would his eyes finally settle and ... blink.

It seemed an effort.

Chris: Can I have a bolus?

I pushed the bolus button. He was alert in a different way these last days or week. The "Can I have a sip?" or "Can I have a cigarette?" or requests of any nature had now disappeared.

Chris: Can you up my dose?

Days earlier I'd called our friend Alan, a pediatric MD. I was worried about toxic levels of morphine, especially in an 80 lb. person. He called a palliative care doctor he knew. Chris was now, after four months, at 160 milligrams per hour plus bolus, and I was scared to inadvertently poison him. The MD told Alan he had no experience with patients using over 100 milligrams per hour. I don't remember having a deep reaction. I had become accustomed to the "never heard of that before" but I think I was shutting down on reactive feelings involving facts or information ... something Chris had long since begun. So ...

Chris: Can you up my dose?
Me: Well, honey, I'm a little worried about going too far ... accidentally.

Usually when denied he'd do with me what couples do ... Face off. But not today.

Chris: (irritated)....."Uhhhnn.....how'd I get in this position?"

I interpreted this to mean the all of it. Contracting AIDS came to my rational thought front. It seemed a strange conversation to have at this time. Nine years in.

Me: Sugar, it's just biology. You didn'...

Chris: That's not what I mean.

He seemed to be talking to himself. I didn't get "position". Maybe the pain?

Me: Uhh, well ... probably 'cause you've graduated from the patches...And you've been on the dose since Janu...

Chris: (irritated) That's not what I mean.

Me: What are...you ... saying?

Chris: You. You won't...I'm stuck with you...in control...and you...won't.

He was voicing something true. I wouldn't. His truth was for me...well, adorable, funny, given the essence of our chemistry, and scary, horrid. In my face was someone who'd lived on into a hard life of agony for fear of letting me go, and for fear of leaving me alone. And in that tiny instant I saw how far he'd fought, endured, and accepted his endurance of an unacceptably reduced self, not for only him, but for the same reason that I wouldn't...the end of our knowable attachment. Each in our own different way, I think, had been incapable of this...more than anything. But at this point anything was bigger. He was far ahead of me, rightfully and understandably. I felt ground moving.

I again shifted back to the rational. The exponential increase at this dose would've been 20 milligrams an hour. Or should it be 25 now? He had a bedsore on his back the size of Chicago. A skinless oval from his ass up to below his "angel" bones.

Me: Well...Let's go up 10 milligrams and see how that goes.

Chris: ..... (I don't recall him saying anything else.)

I did the entry in the drip controller, and in the time it took to do it, he'd fallen back to that strange new kind of sleep. A special sleep that I was confusedly respectful of. I remember feeling odd...and lonely. I spent the day quietly. I don't remember more than to say it was so quiet. And that I knew what he meant. He slept through the whole day. Didn't wake to ask for a bolus or a sip. Ease settled in.

I felt the presence of comatose. I didn't try to wake him. I kissed him goodnight and went alongside his techno-bed, to my bed, or what had been our bed. I was unworried that he would pass in the night. Still I felt that odd, different presence of his. The sense of the place he was at filled the house, just as it had always done. So it was sort of normal. I guess. It made me trust he'd be there in the morning. And, like it or not, Chris was determined. *He let you know.*

Dying now seemed smaller than his obstinance. He had fear, but the distractable fear of a child, easily eclipsed by his strange rage. I knew its arrows, but then I'm someone who knows of things born in him, only for me, because I am me. Someone who found with him a chemistry unpolitical. It made me strong and durable. Like he was. So I fell asleep.

Sparklers

The first time I'd heard of it was around 1979. It was an acquaintance, a friend of a friend known as Tom the Cat, I guess due to his red tabby colored hair and matching big moustache. I didn't know him well. I recall him giving an impassioned speech against the idiocy of being served cold, hard butter pats with warm bread or croissant. Although he was passionately particular, he seemed a nice guy underneath, as long as the butter wasn't ice cold. But we weren't on the same planet, so we remained acquaintances. One day our mutual friend said he was in the hospital. Next thing, he'd died of this weird "gay cancer". It all seemed to happen in a matter of weeks. Thus, I became aware of what we now call HIV/AIDS.

Not long after, my friend John, who was "interplanetary", was experiencing odd health.

He said a doctor told him it was a "tail" of this gay "viral" condition. I had been in a theater group with John. He was an inspirational friend as he'd had less need for logic than I did. I recall his weighty recounting of a dream he'd had: "We were in trouble, in an evil old house with no exit, and suddenly....(smiling) it became California!" Aren't dreams like that? He had a naturally expressive face that twitched without calculation.

He didn't stay in the city very long. Before he left he called one day, sounding very shaky, to ask if he could come up to take a rest after a doctor's visit, as he felt too weak to make it home. He was carrying some medical papers and a rare roast beef sandwich, saying his doc prescribed lots of protein, a rare meat diet. Clearly too weak for even talk, he slowly reclined on the bed. I put the sandwich in the fridge and the damp papers on the kitchen table. I had to leave for work, rehearsal of a prestigious off Broadway production, his dream job. It all seemed unfair. He had a degree in theater. I'd quit high school but was "cute", a "type" with an agent. When I got home he'd gone, leaving a note in a very shaky hand saying thank you. The twice bitten sandwich was left in the fridge.

Soon after, he was living out at his folks on Long Island, and was in and out of the hospital out there. I never made the trek out to visit him in the hospital. Our mutual friend Bill did and would keep me apprised of the dire goings on ... meal trays left outside of his room. (And what other unmet needs?) It was the infancy of AIDS, and people, personnel, were afraid of contact. Bill wasn't afraid, or wouldn't allow himself to abandon his friend. I wasn't as strong. Not so much afraid of contagion as I was (ashamedly) fearful of seeing John deteriorated. Afraid of my applecart getting upset.

His mother wasn't self-fearful. Nor his dad, as far as I could tell. His dad was deaf. On John's 30th birthday, a handful of us friends made the trip out to the family house. John was in a recliner when we entered all "happy" to see him. His facial emotions were bald, more exaggerated. He seemed to have suffered from nerve damage that made this so. There was a box of rubber gloves next to him. He greeted us with a wider range of facial expressions: joy, fear, anxiety. His mom worker bee'd her way around us and managed to lay out an Italian-American brunch, all whilst keeping John serviced. We were a shock to his radically changed world. And hers.

A smoker, I went outside and saw his dad wandering around in the driveway and open garage. He just stared up. Back inside, at the lace table sit-down, we ate sopresatta and cheese and *tried* to be "normal". Inside knowing this might be our last congregation. John, knowing more, was quiet.

Of course, the crown of any birthday is the cake. So Mom delivered one with sparklers on it. But, John recoiled in fear of its prickly violence. And after flashes of joy and surprise, he started to weep. Was is it fear of finality? Or was it that everyone would flee soon? I think it was both. A combo weighted toward the rational fear of sparks, then tempered by a final abandonment by your would be peers.

John dies, where I don't know.

Nice Organ

1986, New York City.

Sound check for the "band" was at 5pm Saturday, as if we needed one. Or as if one would help. Well actually, help might have hurt us, "The Ladies Auxiliary of Avenue A". We specialized in disturbing our material by doing our best, despite not much rehearsal. Representing the overripe and unaware of it, and an "earlier" place in time, our lineup, left to right (for sonic reasons) consisted of four. Our "single" gal, Kay Lester (Lee), on a strident, toe tapping and at times dissonant clarinet. Soprano vocalist and gifted divorcée, Virginia Killinger (Byron) – there's much in a name. Oddball Robin Marshead (Vicky), our percussionist, with her own unique rhythm (late). And bossy Mrs. Terri Cabshawl (me), attempting chord organ.

Featured repertoire? The tried and true gems. "Turkey in the Straw", "King of the Road", a stirring, cymbal driven "Born Free", the room emptying dirge "If Ever I Should Leave You", and spirituals like "Dominique" as well as "dives" into classical fare, like the trebled confrontation of our focused "Flight of the Bumblebee", amongst any others that were in the book Lee had. Only the best band I was or will ever be in. Maybe it wasn't pretty, so? It was magic! At least from where my bossy ass sat.

So, 5pm, we enter the rank, smelly, empty Pyramid Club as our aka selves. I saw Chris there for the first time. He was up on a ladder fixing a spotlight, a jaunty truckin' hat sat askew on his head. He chewed on stir stix and had conflicted eyes, one lazy, like a bored deer. He kept them hidden, and had a blank Sean Penn sneer. He seemed unimpressible, a sound tech. (They seen it all). He disappeared.

On stage, I set my brown plastic chord organ up on a pair of bar stools and plugged my wheezing keyboard in. Suddenly an arm came from behind and tooted a note. "Nice organ" was the flat stix chewed comment. I looked back, and it was he. It wasn't anything but sweet. He disappeared again, and we got down to the serious business of sonic Hi-Fi. At the end of sound check, I saw him, and asked if there was somewhere I could put my organ until the show. I heard myself say it, but too late to stop it. He didn't and did acknowledge the Freudian slip. Blankly, he answered, pointing to a closet where organs were safe, and said, "Be on time". I liked him, and could tell it was mutual despite his social armor.

Like everyone, I'm picky. Okay, maybe dirty stay-outs aren't picky at 3:30am, doin' it with anyone is to never have to pick. The upside is I know what I want, and have faith in it. I can be happy with someone. I consider myself lucky in love. My quarries may be few, and checkered. But I've been loved, and loved back. It's not a boasting matter. I could just as likely be miserable. Doomed by my "picky-ass shit". Or, I could be a happy swingle, known as "Selective984" on the net. But, anything isn't possible. I'm Irish-German, and way too Irish to be bored by myself, gross as that is. So, I'm easily convinced by myself.

Chris was much different, pragmatic and organized. He was driven, but by what? He craved love, viewed sex more as a sport, not some magic that unfolds over time, as I did (in my manual at least). Both can be defenses, ten-foot poles (aw shaddup). His defense was quickly evidenced in that he was, as it turned out, an alcoholic. And I don't use the term lightly. He was one when we met, and for our first year together. It was only our second date when the pragmatist broke through. He showed up shit-faced. It didn't take long for him to cry about it. "I'm a stinkin' drunk!" He sat cross-legged on the bed and delivered this fact with lots of snot and tears.

It was sad, yeah, but more noticeably, it was right to the point. I was falling in love. He most likely thought (or hoped) I was making other plans.

It was just... I couldn't figure how someone who did their laundry so methodically could put up with the self-degradation that's native to the daily reenactments of an active drunk. So after I over-multiplied myself in, the fact would be it would hurt more than just him. And his anger only pointed inward. Plus, he called me "punkin".

He wasn't mean, not deep down where I'd seen. Who is? And well, he was too quick, too remote and jaded, to pretend or sit still in a puddle of abject hopelessness. And me? I looked different with him. My overthinking dreamy complacence was suddenly just that, a yawn beside his direct, albeit, disaster. I felt clumsy, lovable, and stable. He had too much energy, a good deal of it tangled in anger. So he self-medicated. I had hope enough for two. I remember days I'd call to him: "Crispo! Bring that rage over here an' open this stuck window." He'd curse and puff like it was personal 'til it opened. I saw his rage as some useful energy. It didn't scare me. No, he'd have to choose. I already had.

It wasn't an easy first year though. I didn't have any experience with boozing. But I knew enough not to campaign. It was his struggle as to what to deny. I knew if he quit for me, it would screw us up, and neither it nor we would last. And if he quit me, he'd hate the sauce all the more. When he fidgeted in sober daytime, squeaking remorse, I found myself some responses:

1. "..........." the dead quiet (not one I'm proud of...but hey)
2. "You can stop, y'know." (duh)
3. The caring and true: "It's a beast inside you, not you."
4. And cruel challenge: "I dare you to not drink tonight." This one to be applied with a nine-year old's snotty indifference. And rarely. It won't work, but that's the point.

They were all dares. But challenge was what he faced. And anything was better than a tired earful of me droning on of my "disappointments". I didn't do it out of pride, but selfish love. Anyway, he did tell me clearly, up front. I didn't want his honesty turned against him. It's what I liked in the first place.

Yeah, OK, I'd rather have seen his possibility than the disaster that many would see as a fool's gold. I wasn't always so sure, but I never stopped to grow a second head that said, "Maybe leave room for something else". I was happy to keep careful self-investment strategies out of my heart. I'd rather fucking break it. I wish I'd been as risky with other things in life.

Nice Organ

So at last came a day when he made an appointment with a psychotherapist. The man was a Native American working at a community clinic. He told Chris that he lost most of his patients to AA. Chris said that he was friendly, cared, and that he fell asleep from time to time. Once he came home with hand drawn directions to the guy's country house upstate, inviting him to some dinner feast. No, not Thanksgiving. He seemed to view patients the same as co-workers or friends. He didn't employ the understandable separation of shrink and client. Unorthodox methods. I think he was a master of his game. C'mon, if there could be concrete evidence of therapeutic success, this guy had it. He was a soft, raggedy red carpet to the end of an active "Stinkin Drunk".... to AA, and alas, the end of visits to a sleepy genius. He could probably even say "evil-doers" and sound sensible. I hope he knows how good he is.

Butterflies in Attendance

Our wedding was untweakable. Ankle deep in soft silt, in the warm gold sparkle and ripple of a rivulet that ran down to a beach called Lambert's Cove on Martha's Vineyard, two years after we'd met. Nirvana's branch covered entrance was the water's exit into the sea. Splintering out, it twined down in purpled veins over light sand. It stopped once to rejoin as glittery spills into a small salty tide pool near the shore. And, in tide's time, it became the ocean.

We trekked under the branches, upstream to some unannounced magic place. The stream floor was bedded with silky undisturbed silt that loosed itself into cumulous sparkling gold clouds at your foot's trudge, then instantly fell heavily back under the water's clarity. If you didn't know better, it might be mistaken for toxic sludge. Overhead were tendrils of vines on thin tree foliage. To the sides were long grasses, sexy, waving easily from dunes and dark clumps of rock. Further off were patches of loosestrife and distant dark bluffs. All around were scrubby fragrant beach roses. No tables or napkins, no people. Just two misfits in the mist.

Since we hadn't set an exact day or time, we just waited for clear weather. Anyways, it was only to be Christopher Clements and myself, or so we thought. When a fine time came, we made our way to the described rivulet in t-shirts and trunks, to find it occupied by a mass of monarch butterflies fluttering. The island was a first stop in their transcontinental windy life. What more could you ask? They didn't interrupt (that we could tell). Didn't drink'n puke. Maybe they looked better than we did, but who cared? We wound our way up under the thin thicket, with all those monarchs and two $20 silver bands, and no text to acknowledge what was patent to us.

We stopped at some nice anywhere:

Chris: (looking around) All butterflies in attendance?

Me: (looking around) Umm...looks like.

Chris: Could the one on organ stop slaughtering "Endless Love"?

Me: Is that something you can do? (Serious brings out the "Shecky" in me.)

Chris: Uh...OK...Well! ...I just plain love you. Always will.

Me: For my sickness?...or my health?

Chris: (gently, so as to stop my comedy nose dive) Can't have one without the....ba-dum....other.

We said a little more. Not intending anything new, except more. More glimpsing beyond self's suffocation, through each other, come what may. That's marriage...love finds a home in the only someone who loves inside you. So then like anybody's, our two warm fingers penetrated their rings. For us, a thing that acknowledged what already was, without question. Yeah, yeah, OK...y'never know.......and then you do.

We being two males could be seen as "others" in love, making the inclusion of others complex. I'd have needed a hood not to have noticed, and be protective. Anticipations are innate, annoyingly on everyone's behalf. Would we start to question who'd accept us in this? Neither of us wanted to guess about our people. And who wants a "weird" wedding anyway? Or worse, who wants tolerance? What's wonderful for you is somehow wrong or repulsive to others. But when it's your wedding...Fuck that! I say ditch the hoo-hah......So that we did.

a good death

I can't say enough about this approach to a marriage, no matter where it takes place, or whether you're "other". It's all meant for two. Isn't intimate focus what matters? What you take forward? It's what you'll need. And there is honor in need. It's not a circumstance, or an event.

I've noticed there's an exclusion for all of us. Only curiosity cures prejudice. I see us ingrained with prejudice against death. I think it so destructive, as its result is disrespect.

So take speech. Death speech – uhmm... "death" "dead" "mortal" "sad" "fatal" "deceased" "end" "demise" "departed". And grief speech – "gone" "passed" "lost" "delivered(?)" "closure" "mourn" and my favorite ... "laid out".

Tragedy has speech, too (add shock for the unhearing ear) – "torn" "meaningless" "untimely" (there's a schedule?) "brutal" (has its place, but not tied to our forevers) "stolen" "senseless". And the gothic peanut gallery – "doomed" "ghost" "undead" (that's us) "ghoul" "skeleton" "grim swingin' reapers"... for chrissakes, we talk like we've been there. Rest in Peace becomes "R.I.P". Who knows any future? Who should or need "rest"?

This negative terminology = go away. Comfort is not found in dark adages. Is a dread born of dark habit respectful? Isn't the absence of respect what prejudice is?

Is death the greatest of one's earthly achievements?

It's not a circumstance, or an event.

A Good Kick in the Head

Let's get it out of the way. The storm of a "serious" diagnosis. For me, I think this may have been the hardest time. I speak from the perspective of spouse, not patient. For a spouse, it's a diagnosis for you, too. What has been and was meant to be feels suddenly long gone in the face of prognosis *toast*. We don't all go through this. Some of us die in an instant, or with little notice. Some of us get told news. And I don't think that when it comes it diminishes anything, anything except the ground that you've been standing on. A surface which had provided more than you'd ever noticed. Ironically called gravity, it goes, taking orientation with it. An ugly job, but once done, I think it readjusts the senses so that on their return, the unthinkable has magically begun its way into the plausible. Just the same, when that boot hits, it trumps all. And it's not OK.

Chris's kick came in the shoulder actually. On a Monday in December 1991. Cancer, Lymphoma inside the marrow of his left humerus, extending from the elbow up to and possibly involving the shoulder, and possibly ... and possibly ... It started simply enough – sore shoulder in September. "Sounds like bursitis." But somewhere deep inside, I'd suspected, I feared, more. He'd had some peculiar symptoms and episodes during that year. And he was, statistically, a gay man in the late 20th century.

The second boot, Doc Martin steel toe, size thirteen, came the next day...Tuesday, in a phone call to Chris at work. "Well, your HIV tests are in, and you have two problems," said the admirably sunny, optimistic bone oncologist who had performed the deep bone biopsy the previous week. I had seen this man's other side that week before. On the endless day of the endless biopsy procedure.

At 7am, Chris donned a powder blue wrap-around, stupid paper shower cap and goofy foam slippers and went through some beige swinging doors. He was expected to be done by noon. Now, after 5pm, the waiting room had filled and cleared several times over and had all but emptied, leaving just myself and the woman across from me. I'd not met the doctor before. He came out in scrubs and a lab coat calling out to the walls of the large waiting room, with just two of us left in it, waiting for someone. "Clements...Christopher Clements." I stood up and said, "Here." He came over near my chair, to *never* look away from his clipboard.

Me: Hi I'm Joh...

Doc: (to clipboard) Well, he's resting in post-op now. He'll be drowsy. But...um...you can go back now...through those doors. The results should be back by Monday, but...um...bring him down to the fourth floor where my clinic is on your way out. We'll set up an appointment for uh...then. Yeah...Monday...and...um...we'll take it from there. OK!...So we'll see him downstairs in a bit. (Exit)

His demeanor was purposely aloof, extremely cold, anything but sunny. I clearly wasn't to speak. Don't think I could have anyway, because there was no question I'd just been told something profound. Stunned, I looked across to the exhausted looking woman opposite me. She shook her head with worn, unsurprised disapproval and said, "It's a long road", confirming what I'd thought I'd just heard. I said good luck to her as I went toward the doors. Still shaking her head she exhaled a "Good luck to you, honey".

I had all of twenty seconds to snap out of it. Chris was reclining there all damp, groggy and sweet, smiling to see me. "Didn't I tell you?" he said to the nurse, referring to me. This was so fucked. I hated knowing. But I was happy to see him smile. He was feeling no pain, glad it was over, and glad the doctor hadn't come to him as he'd (unknown to Chris) just come to me.

Nurse and I got him street-dressed. Complex, as he had a fancy drainage contraption on his arm, and it was winter. We talked of reward dinner, as he hadn't eaten in 22 hours.

Me: Where's your scarf, gloves? Oops... got'm. (We got him up.) OK, so we just have to stop on the 4th floor on our way out.

Chris: (wide alert, sharply) Who said?

The nurse piped in, "You've gotta make arrangements to get that drainage tube out." She knew. Thank You, Nurse, who ever You are. You could have eyeballed me (now's good a time as any) and walked away, pulling off your rubber gloves. But You didn't. You saw right through me. Your subtle performance skill gave us 15 more priceless minutes of okey dokey.

If only Chris could have gone longer in his doped up relief. When we got to the 4th floor I prayed not to see the doctor, just make the appointment and go. But no..."Hiya guy!

Listen, I need to speak to you, uh...privately for a minute." (clearly referring to me)

Chris: (scared) Well, this is my partn...

Doc: I know, I know, just for a minute. Listen...

As he took Chris whispering distance away, I knew what he was saying, and I knew it was more than just about cancer. Young men commonly don't get this kind of cancer with the exception of HIV. It was something I knew, but didn't say. ("Hey, y'know that cancer you might have? Prob'ly means you have AIDS!") And I never did know if Chris knew before that moment. But he hoped against hope until each result was definite. And who of us wouldn't?

With more than his bubble burst, we walked toward a small room where a deputized phlebotomist awaited. Chris told me the doc had said that the biopsy looked positive and this was commonly seen in HIV, etc. I could only think to say, "I just don't want different train tickets." I'm glad I said that. Blood was drawn from my pale animal. "Okay, Bye." We went to a payphone and called Alan (the same), whose calls had gotten Chris into Sloan Kettering. He was working nearby and came right over with his gentle, stunned, and quiet support, and we shared a strange cab ride back downtown. I think an MD's experience must make intimate illness harder, contrary to common thought.

Any of Us: Oh! I'll call Greg (Friend/MD)!
He may know something.
He may know too much.
Poor Greg.

The next days were floorless. Blurry, although I remember much phone support. Especially Joan's refusal of doom. It helped him.

Monday's follow-up

The bone doctor swept into the room, a burst of sunny energy followed by five or six students, creating a great swirl of white lab coats. He sat down at a desk. They stood and tried not to look sorry, but some did. He announced in an upbeat tone, "Well, the biopsy results are back, and they are positive for large cell lymphoma. This shouldn't be a problem. A course of chemotherapy should take care of it, and then, we'll probably send you over to physical therapy to strengthen that arm of yours. And uhh...(sifting through papers) does anybody have the results on that HIV test? ...Huh?... No? OK, well...we'll be getting back to you on that one. Sooo...I guess there's no point setting anything up until then. (He rises and heads to the door.) So how's the arm feel? Any swelling?"

Chris: No

Doc: Great. Well, I'll be calling you, and we'll set something up then. Whoosh.

I was thankful for his "no problemo" style. Buried in it were "shouldn't be a problem" and "then we'll send you over..." Fixed and shipped. Something to lighten these words that would echo in him.

Thirteen years later, I haven't forgotten one of them. And I wonder what thirteen years of bone cancer management has required him to say, and witness. Now I could see why my gaze was avoided. He did high-energy shows for his patients only. Everyone else got the clipboard. This saved his fuel. His priorities were clean. I'd clean myself elsewhere.

Tuesday's phone call

Chris called me at home from work right after the "two problem" sledgehammer. I said, "Come home now."

"OK, I'm leaving...but what do I say to them here?"

"Say your arm hurts."

On his way home, he saw his friend, Lady Bunny. He just up and told her his twin news.

She said, "Oooh...you're too evil to be destroyed." I'm sure she said it with dismissive certainty. She is genuine. Lookat, when you need a set of brass balls, it really helps to see someone else display them, at your expense, for your benefit. This couldn't stem his anguish, but it was a flashlight back into life's familiar absurdity, a place he could yearn to get back to, eventually. And once you've been kicked in the head, twice, everything can look weird and scary. And Bunny has mastered this.

Our next visit to Sloan

Chris had been moved to another department, endocrinology, and appointed a new doctor, Dr. Strauss. He was doing a study in low vs. high dose chemo for lymphoma and wanted Chris in the study.

At first meeting, his style couldn't have been more different from "happy bones". His diagnostic demeanor wasn't reassurance. It was downright funereal. But he also seemed very focused, and tired. Never to be seen leading a team of residents, he seemed a loner, and maybe lonely, and unpolitical with patients. What all horrors he'd seen were right there in his eyes. His nurse/assistant held him in awe, and was the perfect foil to his Darkula.

She was hands-on, warm, sweet and seven months pregnant. Nothing could have reassured the "diseased" more than her maternal presence. I can't recall her name, as she went on leave shortly after, but she had the gift of sorting out the order of the mess. She leaned forward, gently held Chris's tumored upper arm and said, "We must get rid of this first." Without scaring you, you got the levity and said, "Oh, I see." And you'd ask no further. She could share her calm. It's the gift of some sensitive people. But not all. Not me. Why? Who knows?

Yes, I am sensitive, but it's called "touchy"! And my calmness? That's been me being "complacent". Personally, I think people should back the fuck up! I do perfectly fine without the crummy two cents...Just so you know.

Where was I? Oh, yeah, Dr. David had another devotee, his chemo drip nurse, Anne. Is there a better title than "drip nurse"?

Anne. If someone could make you look forward to chemo, it was Anne. She was a vein-dowsing prodigy. In resemblance and charisma, sort of a Lee Remick.

Commonly tapped by the other skilled arm jabbers, she'd go slide it in somewhere sweet, and then return to hang out. She could have read a book, kept her distance, since a lot of patients may die, but she didn't. Chris missed her after his liberation to remission. I still do. I wish I could describe her better. But, I can't describe a working heart in action, which is the part of anyone you'd really want to explain in detail. Even Anne, pretty as she is, would probably get overly pragmatic (rough on herself), couldn't ever know her beauty. That's what I can't describe.

We were lucky. Chris suddenly had focused foes of the dumb time bomb. Dr. David was a progress man. He published his study. Did treatment protocols change? I hope so, but don't know. He was openly intolerant of shepherding any more than one resident, no flock of interns here. Distract him, make a mistake, and poof, they'd disappear. His personal thing of control was never about controlling Chris or hapless acolytes, just the MuthaFukinCancer! His eagle eye wasn't open out of legal worry. He was schematically involved.

Maybe because he didn't edit himself, he saw stronger, could look a funeral into your eyes, first thing, and get it out of the way. Everybody's thinking it anyway. Smart man. Generous. I was overprotective, inexperienced, understandably needy for answers. Wish I knew then what I...well...I had my job.

Dr. David Strauss, I hope you've found out about the exquisite person you are, even without an explosive foe. I doubt many oncologists could do things as openly as you did, allowing patients space in that clinical setting. Beyond the inferiority.

It never did come back, Chris's cancer.

Denial is Good

My bartending job was in the loud (h'cup) bar of Bandito's, a Mexican restaurant whose gift was the frozen margarita mix and people of all stripes. It was draining, but it suited me, as even for Manhattan the place was liberal, and classless. Gay and straight. No overabundance of honky sistah or poppi. They were all welcome. Depended on you, if you were McPicky, you'd miss its charm. If you needed things catologued, you'd call it sleazy. I thought it was comfortable for the socially secure, insecure, adventurous, and really obnoxious.

Owned by two sweet ungay Chinese dudes who were up in years, and named Jack and Benny, I kid you not. The beautiful absurdities spiraled down from there. If you called in the morning, Jack, a barman from far-gone decades and now majordomo of the house, would answer the phone smoothly, "Hahllow Baahn-dee-taow". Afternoons got you Benny, a long time night porter and #1 human of highest order. Overly apologetic Benny limped on damaged knees from his years toiling behind kitchens (ahh...back of house!) and he spoke even less English than Jack. Benny's phone technique goes unmatched, beginning with what sounds like a 911 audio of a strangulation in progress! "Ay! Ha ngyahh. yah! .. hullo aah .. uhh ...Bah .. uh .. Bahndeeoh!!" The take out menus were mercifully numbered.

My interesting "survival" job was now a taxing thing to survive, given that every third sentence was a question, i.e. "Yo! whatchoo been doin?"

"JohnnAY! How ARE you Doll?"

"Haay Baby! Wussup?" All earnest and deserving a reply. Yeah, people ask out of natural habit, but it's a nice one. I hated lying, pretending, but it often just wasn't the time or place. So I'd plop out the mini skinny every so often in hopes it'd get around. It did. But not always, which was a pleasant reassurance, some will provide you confidence without your asking for it. Anyways, greetings got knowingly truncated.

"Hi Gorgeous!", "Haay Baby! I Love You!", or if they wanted to check in deeper – "So, how You holdin up?... Okay?" People are sweet. It all fell into place, and it was a relatively short time before I didn't fear the "News" stress. I never felt like a sad tragedy or subject of gossip.

One night my close friends, Grant and the aforementioned Alan, his beloved, came in and sat at the bar. It was a welcome relief. I knew they didn't like it there, so it meant that much more. No need to beat around the bush with them. Grant was, at that time, working on an inpatient psych unit in social work. Alan, a pediatrician, ran a family health clinic in the Bronx. Both being gay men through the 80's in NYC, they'd had their share of experience with loss, with AIDS and it's cruelties. But for them, this was close. I recall trying, with dread, to imagine what it was like for them by imagining "what if" it had been them instead of us. But I couldn't. It was an upsetting thing to conjure, and I was upset enough. And, thankfully it wasn't the case. But, before I'd shut down on it, I had peeks into an awful sense of helplessness, sadness.

Yet funnily, somehow in my own real scenario, I didn't feel so helpless and couldn't afford sadness. Sadness like I'd felt at the moment of the "different" train tickets, or waiting during the biopsy. I gravitated to possible goals. Like beating the immediacy of lymphoma. Why even consider HIV? Bigger fish cancer kinda diminutized AIDS. Only denial could keep the truckload of bricks on the truck. If anyone was to be allowed despair it was Chris. But conversely, I was especially determined to minimize his despair, since I felt the mind played a large part in one's survival.

And I loved him. I had no fear of being overbearing, and I can be a controlling know-it-all. Besides, he'd let me know tout suite if my gross cheerleader needed to shut it. Which he never really did. C'mon, if there's ever a time to blindly overestimate yourself – this is it. Should anyone decide you need to wake up and face facts, whatever their motive – tell them to go get their own nightmare, then check back with you. You are putting wagons in circles and awakening any things of power within yourself that you can. These can only be maintained with denial, doom blinders. We know that even the firmest of believers can lose a battle. But when you're putting wagons in circles only an idiot would leave any out. With stakes like these, failure can't linger as an option. And we'd learn about that, should the time come.

So anyway, back at the bar, our discussion brought me to a thought I'd never wondered before right then, at that moment. It just plopped out as a question poised to Grant: "...How can you live without hope?" In his infinite wisdom, and knowing me, he said,

"Well, that's just it, isn't it?" This, to me, was and is the perfect answer. At the time, although it sounded right, it didn't make real sense, not until I thought about it later. You don't.

At some point hope is a choice. Whether you can choose to summon it isn't for shame or pride. It's not in endless supply. It's a fortune! And even a gift cast bountifully, is still a gift, not a given. It struck me that any of us could have no obstacle, excepting hopelessness. Having had my peek, it's not something you choose. If we admire endurance through elusive hope, we offer our distance, disdain, distaste for those that hope jilts. A sad something we think we need employ for our own hope's survival. Deep down we instinctively judge. OK...just remember, self included...we can be fucking ugly. Why choose that? We'll dislike us later, like we can afford it. But there is no currency for this, so at least deny unaffordable smallness, if you can.

Being that all else felt like a dark horse, I was becoming quite friendly with denial. To the point where I saw what I denied...and dispelled it guiltlessly. This helped me morph my natural dreamer persona, my preference for "nice thoughts". Because denial and dreaming, they are cousins somehow. And in order to really help him, I needed my help. So conviction took precedence over fear. And Chris, though Mr.

Pragmatic, had a firm relationship with escapism from his earlier years as an alcoholic, and anger drove him there.

We'd been together for five years, four sober. They were sweet. He wasn't very militant as a reformee. He was strict with himself, not others. He would say so if a boozy social situation bugged him, but it was rare. His drinking buddies drifted away, but for a few. They were sweet people. I knew he missed them. He went to AA a lot and eventually a new therapist. These aren't exactly friendly territories for denial. And for good reason.

In the face of cancer, my cancerian maternal instincts went into overdrive, and his version of denial was to leave things in my hands. I seemed to have an answer for everything, and was good at believing there was one, the one I said. Either way, if I was calm – he could take it to mean all wasn't lost. My antennae were up, and I began to gather information that might hold help.

In the first week of his diagnosis, we went to a mind/body seminar. The guy giving it asked for a volunteer. Up went Chris's good arm. I could see the man zoom in on Chris's eagerness. He called him to come forward and sit in a chair facing the large group of us. The topic was self-hypnosis. The speaker asked

Chris to reveal his ailment, and then his biggest fear, and Chris did.

Then the guy did something very simple. He walked behind the seated Chris and said, "With your eyes, look down at the floor, notice it ... Close your eyes ... Don't speak 'til I open your eyes. Think. Do you remember the last five words you said? Think if you can remember those words exactly. Okay. Now I want you to breathe more slowly and remember what the floor looked like, feel your feet on the picture of it ... fine ... Now think and begin to picture ... the perfect place you'll be in twenty years ... inhale deeply ... notice what I ask. Who are you with ... (lightly resting his hands on C's shoulders) ... good, breathe out ... breathe easy ... as you would ... see ... what's the ground like ... what color is the light? What's straight ahead of you? Notice details ... you can ... alright, perfect ... you feel your feet are resting on this place ... see them ... memorize it now ... you can see again what you saw straight ahead ... the light ... (His hands rose off the shoulders.) Thinkquick! Five Words you Spoke!" SMACK!!! The room jolted at the LOUD hand clap. Chris's eyes popped open. "Hurry, say the five words."

"Uh ... afraid to be ... a burden." Hands on shoulders again.

"Now, I can't scare you again – so close your eyes and tell me what you saw."

"Grass."

"Nice, where is this grass?"

"I'm sitting under a tree, on grass."

Sounds dumb, but a few days later he told me that when he'd start to flip out about it all, this image of the tree would pop into view, interrupting the panic. So Chris went to see this hypno-speaker for a private session. I recall that he wore thick glasses and kept an intense expression on his face. It backfired when he pulled out one of those black and white spiral swirling guns and started intensely swirling it at film noir patient Chris, who burst out laughing, ending the session. He came home and guiltily recounted all. I tried to keep a straight face and remind him he meant well, forgetting that Chris didn't suffer a sanctimonious fool's chiding. He laughed at me as if I were singing "Tomorrow" with the assurance I'd land the role of Annie. I called him an ingrate. As I turned away, I heard him laughing, plain laughter. For the first time in what seemed like forever ago. Swirling guns work.

Advice came via telephone from a friend of a friend. She was a stranger who now wasn't a stranger due to her being in treatment for the same type of cancer. She spoke about welcoming the chemo in to do its work and sucking on ice chips during the drips to prevent mouth sores. Daily tinctures of astragalus and gingko under the tongue to protect the rest of you while cell production shut down to strangle the "umbilical cord" that fed the tumor, which is the action of chemo. She described tumors as dumb and vulnerable, without a personal vendetta. But first and foremost, she said that we should find someone who had achieved remission from the same cancer to meet with. We did, and called him up. I think this is invaluable advice. Nothing else is as concrete. His name was John B.

John B. met us in a café with his boyfriend, also named John. He was like finding a working Pepsi machine in the Sahara. He talked of eating burritos during his chemo drips. "Yeah...ya go bald...yeah, you get tired after awhile." It was like it sorta got in his busy way. He had AIDS, lymphoma, OK, yeah (yawn)...but he was adorable, robust, no bullshit, and someone you'd want to know better. Then he spoke reverently about the checkups that confirmed his continued remission. The possibility of another kick in the head. He had authenticity.

Mental images are powerful, and "live" ones like these can live in you. Remember that with most all things medical, there's a lot of waiting around in fluorescent, colorless places that can't help but send the mind on a conjure, easily negative, since you'd rather be anywhere else. So right when you go squirming, imagining things that may never happen, dry wretching or a central line that can't be gotten in under ten tries – a jaunty burrito pops up. Who'd agree that a neurotic state is physically healthy, or very likely healing.

Denial clears room in the shocked head and soul. Room for images you won't want or need to deny. To feel what you can, and find your own version of all this, and not accept a shit-diploma. Avoid the temptation to think others feel safer admiring your "bravery in the face of "It". They want your success, and you need your version of what appeared as "the inescapable". That's a perspective, or a dramatic adjective, not an ironclad verb. Open that messy head to question preconceptions you had. They were from before.

Screw contempo-speak. Be your own crisis. Find room for the hope you believe in, so you can choose it.

You're living.

That's just it, isn't it?

Audrey Kleenex

Audrey was a professional ass pain, a bureaucrat who ruled the front desk and vibe in the waiting room of the "imaging" center that a couple $mart radiologists opened near Sloan Kettering. And a slew of other local medical sites. From 1st Avenue over to York Avenue between 62nd and 80th Street lay this host of high-end institutions, commonly called Hospitalville. We called it the "Sick Riviera". Even these renowned hospitals have only so many scanners and too many orders, so they farm it out.

Audrey lurked resentfully over the goings on. You'd get your scan, but only after Audrey made you feel bad about it, and her involvement in it. Her demonic software scheduled seats aboard flights into the inner battle between hope and dread, the results. If you needed a ticket you'd have to face her first. She had a disappointed way of looking at you that said, "Aren't you dead *yet*?" Her put-upon style of tapping at the keyboard never wavered from exhausted disgust at your pathetic nearness...in this she was dependable. It was so obnoxious it was funny, until you watched someone else face her. Like an older couple, ashen lady in turban, no brows, hubby at her side, in over his head. "Are you telling me you don't have ONE credit card?!" If you didn't work hard, your blood would boil. She must have spent years in the bowels of some last ditch "debt collection" trailer, getting called "bitch!" and getting hung up on, getting hard, polishing her "style". She was a deep purple 40-ish lesion, and an indispensable lesson.

Chris had good insurance. (This was before the messy onset of HMO's). Didn't impress her though. Nothing did.

Audrey: Only got Thursday 8am ... (sigh) ... I *need* a credit card #.

Never give them this. Ever. You'll *need* it later.

'Cause they'll swipe that card through, and good luck getting those thousands (that you probably don't have) back. "I've got your number" took on new meaning. She never got mine. I'd already learned the hard way.

Audrey Kleenex

I'm not nursing a grudge. I'd just never seen anything like it. And even now, years later, having seen a lot, her twisted behavior, the horror of it, stands the test of time.

Yeah, sure, Audrey found it distasteful, having to take it out on the terrified, usually old and visibly afflicted. But her response to this inner pickle was to relish it. Our theory was that Audrey needed a different job, though I thought she was unemployable. We'd stifle our own naughty laughter at the sight of her "power lurk". Could there be a who whom she'd chance a rusty "nice" on?

Since my role here wasn't drinking two quarts of metallic cranberry stuff and lying still so as to image clearly my possible demise or reprieve, my role became keeping Chris away from Audrey...and waiting. Yes, plenty of time to observe her fundamental disdain of those forced to face her punitive skills. If it had been me bringing, say, my elderly mother, they'd still be trying to figure out how to reconstruct her face, but it was Chris, who could behave on the edge, treat her as though she didn't exist, get what he needed and then forget about her. Satisfied, in that he knew she knew his knowing this ate at her. His rage trumped hers and made him confident. To him, she was just another drag queen desperate for attention that could never be had.

One night, post diagnosis, he repeatedly smashed a metal folding chair into the floor, bending and breaking it. It came out of nowhere. So, I thought less contact with Audrey was a good idea. Since all his detached self-control at her gross behavior was just his mask for rage. He didn't want interaction, just my scan "lady" as he called her. But why chance it? So I dealt with everything at the desk that didn't require his signature.

I began to understand there were likely going to be more scholars of baditude in the health care world, and that they weren't real good places to unload your rage. No matter how hard they begged a challenge. These folk don't lose battles, 'cause this is how they see each oncoming face. They want to fight, and they confuse their unmet needs with the little power they have. Don't we all at some point? Anyways...I never saw anyone rewarded for challenging old Audrey. Quite the opposite. She had that rotten thing. I'd call it a serial helpless need to project self-loathing on cancer patients. Or "How to Win and Keep That Losing Streak". When bookstores open a "self-hurt" section I may be induced to chase her down to pontificate a purplish book.

Sad fulfillments propel these destructive identities. Lots of people need to get out of health care but can't. So, I'd come to see it as though they illuminated the unwell in a preferable light. The sick get tired of being the pitiful ones. Not everyone is a congenital whiner, y'know. Your body might be fucked but at least you're not them. Maybe this sad ilk could help after all, with a warning label. A sign over the desk or worn round the neck: "At Least You're Not Me!"

When I couldn't see things this way, excuses wouldn't hold. But strangely, and probably alone: **"I'd Like to Thank Audrey"** for the lesson. Like she could care.

However, one day, even Audrey giving Pat Robertson the treatment couldn't have distracted me. At Sloan, if you had a temp over 101°, you had to come into the emergency room. We did this on many occasions, be it 4am or whenever. This consisted of a saline drip, blood work for white cell count and a chest x-ray. On this day, Chris was passed out fever style on a rolling cart as we waited in the x-ray waiting room. I was tired and nervous about some impending scan results, and he was safely unaware of me. I cracked and started to cry, well ... weep ... uncontrollably. Kinda hysterically. It's not something I'd done. It heaved deep, and went on. Matter of fact, it got worse as it went on. My throat was frightening everyone. There weren't enough kleenex in the tri-state region for this monsoon, and I didn't even have even one. So I graduated from my sleeves to his sheet. I would've been wishing to stop it, for the others that were there. But...there it all was, unavoidable...him, out of contact, in some inescapable danger.

Then an Middle Eastern guy about my age who'd been pampering his cancered father came over with some tissues. Wordlessly offering the little cello-pack, he took a respectful and scared look into my eyes. His eyes said, "I'm terrified of this, what you're doing. It might be me one day. Will facing you help? Mostly...I'm sorry for you now." I nodded. Then helplessly continued my choked wail. By croaking alarming sound effects at involuntarily volumes.

The open raw humanity in his daring decision to approach my hysterical freak show, upended any assumptions of interpersonal possibility. Religions and cultures seemed dry snacks for groups, and stupid beside his singular facial expression with kleenex extended. It felt like the first time I had been spoken to. His optic communication was human. Unselfish concern overcoming deeper fears, the spirit of you as me. And curiosity of what Chris and I silently contemplated. Separation.

He could have wheeled his dad into the hall. Certainly everything in this context instinctually encouraged him to do just that. But he didn't. He was curious about the event, and drawn like a zombie to see in, and show he feared as much. Maybe he'd been here before. I don't know. We never spoke. I never broke like that again. But I'm glad for having done it, and more surely for his intrepid majesty.

But it couldn't stop my overdue, loud and gooey storm. Only my role/duty at Chris's wakening for the x-ray could smack me back out into control. Me crying like that could needlessly spell failure to him.

Was this my fate? When the day came that he wouldn't "wake"? And I wasn't to hear "new" him again? Was this cathartic heaving what missing him would be like? How could I move? Seeing a life of masking what I couldn't contain, just to get by? My natural innate self-preservations, okay? I'm not ashamed. You can't deny the self and expect to be effective. Anyway self wasn't the big deal.

He was.

How could Chris get out safely? Without cathartic agony? This is what I had allowed to the surface and responded to in kind.

These fears never materialized.

But back then I had no images otherwise. What I'd seen was a list of what he'd never want. And so became things I wouldn't allow, not if I could help it. What could I change in this, being realistic? Not what I feared. Unless that could change.

So the way I saw, and what I took in changed. I had supposed much of this to be subconscious, 'til I saw that *that* don't mean shit when you're up against it.

If all this reads as indulgent, it is, and OK, I am. And you? You are either blissfully inexperienced (enjoy it, really), have lost interest in my voice, have forgotten that this isn't a work of fiction, or you're employing denial effectively (you go!). I intend to expose myself, so as to give you something to make an opinion of. Learn to decide how you want, or don't want things. Based on judging me, and the beans I spill.

I don't like writing this. I'd learned to go get a concept of a good death from witnessing other people's experience in dying. People were all around me in the late 80's through the 90's. So I saw. People who I thought died in less than what could have been, purely because of death's gray identity. I learned it in 3-D, in real time. But since I can't reanimate that for you, we're stuck with my messy head.

It Became California

In late September, after he'd recovered strength and hair, after he'd established what minimal plans there were to be had back then with his possibly inspired (but by what?) HIV doctor, we went on a trip, a reward trip to San Francisco and a tour north of it.

In San Francisco, we spent time with my very close friend, Joe, and his partner of twenty some years, George, relationships formed when I was a teen in my hometown of Buffalo, New York. We saw David, also from Buffalo, who was very sick with AIDS and had lost his partner the previous year.

David lived up on one of those steep wooden stepped and gardened hills and had us up to meet his sweet dog and visit the several shakily filled pots of ash on the mantle, that'd been his spouse. Driving in the car I remember him saying, "It got in his brain the doctors said, and that there was nothing they could do...(long pause)...now it's so...quiet." He wasn't going to stay around long. They'd been a couple, a family, for a long time, and though it seemed wrong he should endure his young exit alone, he wasn't alone. There was their dog. He didn't lack in dedicated friends. He didn't mention his family. Maybe there was nothing to mention. I figure there's a crap load of parents who cut out on their offspring in the first 15 years of AIDS, and are now approaching their own mortality, measuring themselves and dreading some imaginary bill to pay for having been weak. And too, a crap load of parents who look ahead, hopefully. And some that never recovered and blew their brains out in the garage.

I could sense David's independence, his freedom. I think he'd had enough change and wanted the household to take its natural course as an internal structure, not up for others' discussion. Y'now, for better or worse. A family. Not long after our visit, Joe called to say David had died at home. As he often didn't answer the phone, his friends respected this. So he hadn't been found until some days after. That sweet dog was trapped unfed ... almost ... oh, y'know ... other stuff. Unthinkable details. I don't know. Just don't ever talk to me about "traditional family values". I'll instantly hear the last word in that verbal baseball bat and know that you're cheap.

To my knowledge, "traditional" is a furniture style at Ethan Allen (probably discontinued), or an old tune with no author named. Is it now a "lifestyle"? Is it superior? Or self-absorbed? And anyway "lifestyle"... I don't know what the hell that is. Being gay isn't a "lifestyle". Like we gays all lurk in public toilets and "trysssting" places. Aww, eat me. Yeah, some do. Like some straight guys don't hopelessly hoot at uninterested women or get up to gooey shenanigans under their toupees 'n trench coats in XXX booths? You know, the tragic stereotypes, they go round and round. "Lifestyle" (conservative in origin) is a rude, condescending code word for a stereotype. And "Lifestyles", ironically, is a condom manufacturer who grabbed the market from the longtime underused old favorite – "Trojan" (code: big one). Stereotypes are pervasive, beyond persona. Death gets it right in the nose. So, a guy living a "gay lifesyle" succumbs to the ravages of AIDS, expires unattended at home, and is partially eaten by his dog.

For me, David took control of his household, and I admire him in his strength. He seemed in touch with something good to come. Of all the friends' deaths I recall, I think of his as having been a good one. Sitting up in their place, he was so relaxed, fearless and uncornered. After a Chinese water torture of bad breaks, he had control. I really recall his radiance.

We drove north, around Bodega Bay up to Jenner and its sea lions, and then inland to the giant redwood groves. Then we went to see our friend's mother. She lived on a swell ranch outside Sonoma. We arrived at the large protective fence in our rental car. There was the sound of very old folks, having loud, slow orgasms. It turned out to be just that, two big exotic box turtles that she keeps for her son, doing what we do with each other. They mowed the smallish lawn around her trellises by eating the grass on a slow but consistent basis (well, almost constant). The rest of the place seemed to be tar grass and casual untied horses with a creek and hills with clusters of oaks that looked out for miles.

Forget the magic ranch, it was she, Marilyn, who took our breath. She was on one level, practical. But, free of the Headset that drives the practical. She was a sweet host, but it was her spirit, or something I can't describe, that made me want to be around her, soak her up. Chris was crazy about her, too. Excursions from the ranch were fun. We'd be driving up along some rocky promontory, but... "What is Marilyn up to?" It didn't feel nosey, just concerned that she felt included. Nature's scenery, or art, is a taste of another spirit. We see or feel it embodied in these places and their expressions, but it's just not the same. We were two animals. Only the animal's presence can create the chemical foot on the pedal that gives us reason. She exemplified this, eclipsing the surroundings. And helped me see how I saw Chris. I don't understand it. I don't know that I should, or even need to comprehend it. But I know enough to "know" it anyway.

On return to San Francisco, Joe and George hosted a cookout in our honor. Other Buffalonians were there along with Cali's they'd friended and I'd met. Chris was unparalleled in being uncool, and cool with no one and everyone. He didn't have "along for the ride issues". It was all a ride. I admired this innate way of his. Not like he had no ego, just an egoless take on any "social" event. He was as they say in the creative worlds, a tech, those who toil in the arts but are really and rarely considered creative. An insult, a stupid absurdity that goes back before the Hatfields and McCoys. And bears a scary resemblance.

Techs don't need the "center" of attention, but it'd be nice if those lit centers behaved as if they understood who and what holds them effectively in place, and that it takes just as much instinct, finesse and yes, phoning it in, to be an "operator". But Chris was a gay tech. Which gave him social running papers. Neither one of the guys, nor a star wannabe. Though he eventually experienced raw public disaster as he lost his cherished organizational skill, he'd known how good he was.

He wasn't in it for the compliments. Oh, he hated the clown suit of failure, but equally hated owning the sabotage of others' work, not enough to stoop to excuses, but beyond this he was uniquely immune to others' opinions. I saw how true this was from the rare persons who produced a shameless sweaty desperation in him to impress them. Hoping to relate, or at least not repulse them.

These few bright, clearly original queenie types, always withheld though, only to get trapped in their icicles. They held the upper hand and his unwanted adoration, but were somewhere unwilling to part with the nuisance of his pathetic association. I never did ask him or them: "What's up with the scary fan shit?", in case it was real and thereby a touchy subject. I never did know if he really needed their repeated disapproval, or was cruelly baiting their inner narcissist to dull their sparkle. If so, it worked. But then he was a rotten liar. And these four leaf clovers aside, he was plain unimpressed. If you had hard info you'd share it. Must have been cool finding it.

His idea of reading a book was a map, atlas, or manual. Most anything else would get the small, unintended eye roll of inconsequence. Like he'd seen the gamut of fools tripping on their indulgences. But born knowing we're all in the show. Fighting it just gets you a follow spot. And will empty the room.

I was quietly worried about my friend Joe's health, little stuff, but particular little stuff. AIDS stuff. He confirmed my fears in a letter that came after we got home. He said he didn't want to ruin our trip and that he was afraid to say it in person. He was an odd lightening bolt, and George was a seemingly mellower sunbath. Joe didn't live long, but died as hard as he lived. Not two years later he contracted PML. Basically, the brain eats itself. George kept him home, eventually tied to the bed, for the five months he lived into it. Those barbecue friends took turns filling in when George went to work and Ryan White funds didn't cover. Cal-Med ain't all it's cracked up to be.

This took a toll on George. Five years later he took his own healthy life in a rental car parked in a hospital lot. He never spoke of such an idea. He was fatally quiet about being crushed. A shock and a mystery to his friends. But not really. One close friend set her feelings and anger down and said, "He tried so hard, no one can know. He put on one helluva show, a real trooper. He just ran out of reasons, I guess." I wonder if they *both* died undermedicated.

I miss the infamous Joe Breeze. He had the guts to tell you what he perceived, and enjoyed an equal response regarding himself. We were kindred oddballs from nowhere, and we'd loved it. A hard thing to enjoy on your own. Like most things. And George, I miss so much. We had so much in common here.

Not long after our return, Chris started an anti-viral. A week later he said he felt funny, overanxious. Well, it wasn't long before he was spiraling into an episode of mania. I didn't know what this was, or eventually, who he was. It was him, but off the register. I'd no concept of bipolar disorder. This wild ride went on for about three months till his MD called and said Chris was in his office and had just flung his credit cards at the Doc. "Has he been abusive?"

Me: Well, he's been sleepless, irritated, rude, and irrational.

Doc: I'm checking him into the psych unit. I've seen this before.

That day I took him to psych admissions. The admitting MD was helpful to him. Said what he'd prescribe and what signing in meant. Elevator up to heavy metal locked "ward". Inside was a paucity of working light bulbs, occasional blinkering flourescents. Oops. Hello Hell. Chris was all anti-authority and stuck his tongue out at a security guard who'd been eyeballing him. The guy hissed at him like a snake. All I could think of was his brittle upper arm bone. They gave him a d-d-dose of Haldol, and he was sleepy as they bounced me. I called his therapist who said, "We can't help him now." I wasn't on that boat. The next day he was back. The Chris I knew before. It had been longer than I realized. We wrote the 72-hour letter to get him released. I was afraid they'd break his arm, or his spirit. But, it was the start of a long battle with bipolar disorder. It often eclipsed his HIV, and our relationship.

I faced an ugly thing. To do for him, with his coaxed agreement, instead of with him. I never imagined this. I never considered abandoning him. But now it was different. You either must, or you can't, no in-betweens. Who can say? Who cares what's said. You're in it or out. And once you're in, it matters a great deal how things get done. For both of you. Basically,

I reshaped, hoping for the best, but the best was changing all the time.

My expectations and my idealism were taking a beating. Along with my ego. His was all over the map it seemed, and I was becoming a security guard, and a doormat. No one could want this, or I'd hope they don't. But it turned out I could do it. I'm sure from any other vantage point I looked taken to the bank, but I think I was my strongest. To think back on what I maintained, while foregoing normalcy, or even the remote sense of it. Not only I, but we, endured. No one else could make it happen. It was the job. If people can die for their country, I should shut up. On the other hand, go live with your own beloved's bipolar reality, and check back with me. I certainly don't know how to want to, but I must have because I did. I think somehow Marilyn helped make it seem reasonable to subjugate oneself for the other.

88 Stairs

I'd been sprawled out on the landing of the stairwell for I don't know how long. The white posts, long shiny teardrops with square bases, supported an ebony banister. Up overhead, a ceiling of long dripping Spanish stucco wound around and went up to a third floor. Down below stretched a forever of endless swirls of golden ribbon shapes on brown. Linoleum that looked real palatial, even up close. In the air? Franz Liszt, Chopin, or Rachmaninoff echoed through me and the stairwell, completing my mental transport into magic, giving Buffalo's blah daylight deep meaning and colors. My hands animated the figures around the white columns with heavy dialogue. ("Begone!" or "Hurry Backeth To Me!") My figures were Lords and Ladies, despite their tawdry lineage.

The Lords were plastic army "men", and the Ladies were kleenex clipped to hair rollers.

Below I saw her hunched and troubled form go into the living room, so I hurried down the stairs. She'd fallen onto the sofa, sobbing, "I just don't know what is wrong with me!?!" I knelt and petted her soft, upset face. I was near four years old. My Mother, a kindred dreamer and #1 DJ, she had a bum thyroid. I couldn't know. I just wanted to help, and she made me feel I did, by letting me try. This is the clean gift lost hearts give. She gave me trust to serve my love, spouse, call it what you want. A parent is innately protective of a child. A love is protective, and innate about their beloved. Or is there a difference?

Forty years later, October 18, 1999

Dad: Hello.
Me: Hi Dad, it's John.
Dad: Well! If it isn't John. You're just in time. Mother's resting here, but I know she's anxious to speak to you, so here she is.

Dad had sped a blue, breathless Mom to the emergency room two days earlier. They brought her back in triage. So now, after ICU, she's got a room with a phone.

Me: Happy Birthday, Mom.

Mom: John! Oh! (laughing) Can you believe it? Dad and Tom and Jean and oh...Teresa and Fran and Karen and Joey and Christine all came by tonight! And I'm thinking ... Oh! ... Today you may have been going to my funeral! And just think, here we are in the hospital! ... Celebrating! ... Ohh! ... Isn't that funny, John?

Me: Hysterical, Mom...and you got laughs with that one?

Mom: Ooh, you, you're funny. No, really John, I mean...I've been so blessed, a wonderful life....And Dad. Oh! All of you children, grand and great-grandchildren. I tell ya ... I'm ready to go, doesn't worry me in the least. I mean really...John...C'mon, I'm 81! Can you believe it? Oooh! Poor Dad, I was a goner. But you'll never belie...

I believed it. And that she was up on prednisone. Five years later she still easily dismisses disaster with a breezy, "Oh...well...that's that." Others' interpretations are, to her, theirs. She's got what I'd call, accidental balls.

She had a strange youth, an only child boarded in a convent where few boarded. Her maternal gifts brought her adult life another isolation, bore 'n raised eight kids who worship her. Worship is nice, but she preferred interacting with us, and stayed on our level. I know all eight of us felt protective towards her earlier than kids normally would. She's stayed a young spirit. And we've each, in our own ways, kind of grown old on her.

When my caring for Chris came, a lot of it came from her. Now I see a younger spirit present in me, having run hard, having stretched myself (at times unwillingly), having loved. I'm younger than when I was younger.

My mother, to me, is perfect. Some may see her sweets as daffy, weird, idealistic or even superficial. I see her as a wet slap in the face of gravity. With her, something bad is actually marvelous after all! And once she gets the thread, she'll weave her curious logic for you, no charge. Her brown beagle eyes gaze sometimes too humbly. Solemnly she'll invoke: "God's Hand! Isn't it so beautiful?" She knows she'll get a hard time from me here. Not that I disagree, I'd just rather not agree on "God", even with her. Some may shrink at her enthusiasm. She is a delicate thing that accidentally spooks tough people. The more delicate the bloom, the stronger the frame.

I think we gel because of things in these paragraphs, because of being her youngest, because she wants to know me, not control me. I'm my problem. She always saw my possibility, despite me. Me? I'm awed by her pluck and the shameless slapstick that life's boredom goads her to provide. To control her may look simple. But it's impossible. To even want to try would be repugnant, and useless.

February 2005

Yet, as it turns out, I have more in common with my father than I'd ever thought. Recently I visited them, saw him maniacally filling her weekly pillbox and attending to her every need. In him I saw myself, five years ago. Things about us that once had us on different planets now seemed identical. We have more in common than I, or he, could've seen. I've known what he faces.

He's known a lot of loss, but I'm his only son who's lost his beloved to death. When he spoke, I needed to know what he felt. When I spoke, he listened, wanting to hear. This was more than we had done in all our years. I think we are at last, fortunate friends.

I recall back when I was searching for an apartment in NYC for Chris and me, as he couldn't get up our six steep flights, no elevator, 88 steps, or three steps for that matter. We went step by step. It was a formidable scenario. Finding affordable wheelchair accessible apartments in NYC seemed hopeless.

I got a letter from Dad and Mom: "You're both welcome to come and live in our house." No ifs, ands or buts. They were in their late seventies. They knew it could mean things. I was speechless. Moreover, I knew that Dad knew he couldn't guess what horrors AIDS may bring, and still he offered him, his home and delicate wife/my Mom, to shelter us, whoever we are, knowing they'd witness Chris and me, their son, in all our complexities.

So for the second time, since Mr. Kleenex, I cried. My folks had touched what anyone's God hopes to inspire. They are parents who, in practicing their faith, Catholicism, overcame what "us" was, so as to help. I felt for us, only love. Over time, it had been for Chris and me to show ourselves, albeit carefully, to be seen. But then, it was them, and their faith, who sent a letter, with such a selfless and brave offer.

What can faith bring?

Saint Plops

As I write this suggestion to rethink death, the country is at war going on three years, many limbs and lives lost on all fronts. And I fought so hard for one life. And having battled a biology, it's very hard to accept ideology as a life-taking entity. I watch TV news that shows all the faces and names, lives (American anyway) given, that would be PBS. I canceled my cable. Six figure pancaked toads makin' hay and not even a credit? Outta my way "Info-Bimbo's", or what my sister Karen referred to as "plops", after walking her huge sheepdog.

Watching my someone go slowly, I can't imagine losing them suddenly, at a distance. But, having endured the quiet, I shut my mouth. Joining quiet gets hope in me for the "us" left here. I fear their rage and doubts. If we "knew" rationally that death is an instant, a birth we're just not privy to, maybe we'd know it emotionally, later, and would unburden "our lost" of our hurt. This, survivor, is something that is yours. By right. You're left to deal? Well everyone else can shove it, including the departed. But eventually, if your roof crushed you right this second, would another's pain soothe you? No. I know the aorta's nasty snap. Mine not Yours? Different bus, same destination: "The Quiet".

Slowly I descended into being the person behind the wheelchair, a gross cheerleader, in charge of poo and pee, a reflecting pool of burden. My "Quiet" didn't come home with a flag on it. But it came. And from it emerged a deeper version of my Chris, though I couldn't always see him. In fairness, I wasn't always seen. My rewards can't be seen by others, despairingly. You'll seem to you, a worm, to others a tedious Saint Plops.

One Wednesday

Every day can't be like this one was. That this one was possible at all is profound for me. A late summer day. Chris had withered so. His new and newer anti-retroviral treatments had been giving decent blood work results for months, but he was disassembling regardless. The numbers had ceased to matter. What had once been a hard won and useful gift, now...just wasn't. So on this particular afternoon, it shook me out from my rat wheel and onto the shredded newsprint of shrunken choiceless run tunnels. If you could, you'd see the freedom.

He was propped in one of the several of the rotating bedsore avoidance positions on his recliner. Pillows defended unpliant knees from each other. A special gel cushion did its best under the squared hollow areas that used to host his cute butt. Gravity crushes the bony house in on itself. Armadas of soiled pillow things escort you, and identify you, or not. Depends on you.

Magically, a front tooth (having quietly come out) tumbled from his slim alien hand onto the tray table, and then he instantly refocused in on Judge Judy. Not a word. Complete unimportance. For him the tooth, for me Judge Judy.

His limited interest in vanity amounted now to an impenetrable boredom. The other front tooth had fallen out a month or two ago, in fact many had gone now, giving his bony faced smile a sort of slapstick vaudeville charm. I loved the variations on those slow smiles. *The Unsure* (should this be funny, or is it 'cause I'm a disaster and it shouldn't be, thus has balls and is?), *The Surprised*, annoyingly hard to get, especially next to that old sure thing, *"Look! A Puppy!"*

OK, I've noted my two loves have overwhelmingly preferred dogs and me, over people. But it's a high compliment, given that I see myself as a diplomatic over-thinker, which I find gross. It's hard for me to see any charm in that. Dogs don't give a shit, or if you're ailing, they don't stare. Chris loathed pity to the point that he eventually enjoyed strangers' discomfort or sorrow at the sight of him. He said, "Well, if they can't enjoy it. Somebody should. They look stupid."

So, I'm thinking about the tooth, and the impending PILE of afternoon pills. The rooms loomed, doomed to the strained strains of loud Judgey Judy.

I say, "Honey, you never have to go to the hospital again."

What a smile I got. Moms Mabley would've stolen it. It was just common sense. I got the pill box, "And well, what do you think about each of these meds?" He'd thought about them alright. He was the one who'd been taking them and their side effects. I called the doctor to say he was stopping treatment excepting anti-bacterials and a stool softener. There wasn't much resistance. The nice thing was that, with all respect MDs are due, their opinion wouldn't have mattered. This was a family affair. You don't live for your doctor. It would be a rude burden to affix that to them anyways. And, if they didn't agree, it's their duty and right to say as much. They aren't gods or quacks. They are people. They consult and direct with their hard won knowledge, sweating at the edge of a society that is capitalistic. We don't deny it. But proclamation don't mean our system "democracy" is all that groovy, free, good, or bad.

It's just all pointless, on say, a Wednesday, when a tooth opens you.

So, after unloading hospital fears, 10-15 pills, four times a day, and a psychic high-wire routine, we were on the same page for the first time in what seemed forever. So, throwing all caution to the wind, I got someone to cover me and took the night off of work. Wild man, huh?

Me: Where should we go?

He: To the boats.

So I packed up Chris and his new come-apart, transportable "quickie" wheelchair into our rusty Subaru, and drove down the West Side Highway to the boat basin at Battery Park. Reassembled and propped into his self-controlled module, he sped off for a bit of speedy Nascar motorchairing, then came vrooming back. Where to go? We went to this big outdoor café with umbrellas, demi-trees, and fake stone grounds alongside these cheesy fiberglass yachty looking crafts parked in this little harbor. Y'know, kinda Scarface/SUV boats.

They would have looked out of place in New York, except so did everything else here. But for the old sea wall and the roiling Hudson River sploshing around against it, it felt like a Mall Food Court. OK, there were a couple actual wooden boats, which made Chris ease off the contemptuous authentic old salt routine. At least 'til one of the fiber-coke investa-floats treated us all to an entire Hootie & Blowfish CD. **Real loud!** But...there was a nice breeze, and we were on an adventure. Maybe they were having fun on that ugly boat anyways. After all, we were ugly, and fun we were having. Yeah, of course it was tinged.

So to the outdoor food "court".

Chris ordered an iced tea and raw oysters, normally an immuno no-no. I squelched my usual "ix-nay". He only ate one anyway. Then he lit a cigarette!!! About 50 feet away, no joke, sat a couple with their baby in a mega-stroller. This smoke miasma, or rude anachronism on Chris's part, seemed to drive the wife over the edge, into just the attention getter she'd needed. Lots of frowning and hand wafting in sour horror. I focused in – she was trying to get Mr. Husband-Tired-of-Long-Day-at-Blah-Blah-Biz to *do* something! He had a leg up on a chair and seemed drained, immune to her toad attack and wishing his cell phone would ring.

She summoned the waiter. The husband looks over at us and turns back with a downward headshake. The waiter backs away, taking a cue from the Mister. Now, I'm sympathetic, aware of the isolation that mothers get thrust into with young'uns, but Who the Fuck was she to look at him and see a cigarette! Want to edit him! As if her sad ass space could be tweaked into somewhere nice with her still in it? I wanted to put the cigarette out on her furrowed forehead. My rage was as big as my joy had been. I should have been watching the water, but maybe it's wise to meet a representative of who you'd never want to be when you're faced with being just that. Or even better, maybe we'd wind up on Judge Judy!

"SIR! That does NOT give you the right to "skweeze" her COBB SALAD with your FIST! Whack! Judgement for the plaintiff in the amount of $15.95! plus tax and tip!"

Chris was unaware of this embarrassment unfolding behind him. I just told him under no circumstance was he to extinguish the Marlboro Light. I should have told him to turn his "quickie" for the show. He'd have called it a hoot. But he was watching the water. He could care less. Besides, it was before the smoking laws, and he was the last person within 80 blocks who needed tips on defending himself, no matter how ill. Of course, no one said anything. "Hey, could you put that out please?" Good luck! I'd battled his rage. But now I was proud of the obstinate creature he'd inspired, a ferocious me. I'd seen and been the object of his degradations, self-consumptions...and yet, he never looked down towards others.

No, not like I had just done.

Chris was never admitted to the hospital again.

To the surprise of many, and I'd imagine some well meant hopes to the contrary, he lived on for almost one year more. For all the peace I have with him, I do wish I'd spawned a couple more spontaneous Wednesdays. But I don't think they define life more than any other day.

Tarantula

somebody say the sky is the limit
but of what? god and i don't know.
not since we've endured the endless hour
by its minutes   incapable and
                    inescapable
when it's you stuck in its traffic
turns around 'n round and leaves to leave you
nothing left of you to recognize   crawl up on
me baby
spinning in doubt about a doubt you're
spinning yourself
into a tarantula.....
or... butterfly who changes

they say the wind has no sin ...no beginning
and no end
oh well you and i we should live in it with no
beginning and no end

a good death

your tracks they burn the ground and leave me
nothing left
to conceive in you scream at me spitting and
cursing my help and my helplessness
but i know you   *you need*
'n you know me   *I need too*
crawl up on me baby
have faith in the faith in you
and the the sky is the limit
say the sky
say the sky
say the sky

The Beautiful Time

As I sat in Grant's office and thought about the state of things, things weren't in control. I wasn't as ready to admit it as needing to scream it. Grant's busy, papered desk of work was uncomfortably located in a locked ward of the psych unit where Chris was again a patient for his fourth stay. I sat at my good friend's desk and saw how our "outpatient" efforts weren't meeting the situation's needs. Chris's bipolar disorder had graduated to what they call a "mixed state", or manic and depressed at the same time. Translated: "I should kill myself" mixed with "AND IT'LL BE GREAT!"

About a year before this we'd joined a couple's therapy group at GMHC. With all the best intentions, it didn't work. Chris's bipolar behavior dwarfed his HIV and odd-balled him in the group. He loved playing "evil brat" to my "saint" or "poor thing". I hated that. I didn't understand his need for a sense of self-determination beyond my controlling, clucking hen. I was sick of being fought by him, being the warden that I felt impelled to become. Grant suggested I should get a therapist of my own, and with his help I did.

For the next two-and-a-half years my therapist was Steven. I arrived with a goal: not to fail Chris. I asked him if he had experience with loss, a situation like this. He said no and offered to refer me to someone who did if I wanted. But I didn't. He seemed durable, something you'd need in this.

I began to feel certain ways, before and after the sessions. In the beginning I felt as though I weighed a ton whenever I left. Then for a while it was a weatherless city of sad, beaten faces on the way there. Ultimately, they're about you, not the situation. Not an easy job, Stephen did good.

It was in this frame of reference that I was struck by the change. People looked happy, and there was weather, great winter days. I felt creative, inspired. I didn't feel guilty that Chris was gaunt and bed-bound as I walked in appreciation of things. His anger toward me had subsided. Now he took in my mood, as he shifted onto one foot here, one foot extended to somewhere else. Neither seemed wrong. I may have looked bonkers. I don't know, and don't know, and don't care, as long as I don't hear about it. I am still earthy. And this territory is tender as you get. Try it 'n see.

Creatures/Crayons

All of us are good at some things, not all things. Someone refers to you as a creature and, depending on the variables, this is taken as good or bad. Was it modified by a "lovely" or "useless"? Are you "good" at taking insult, or "bad" at understanding that the intention is theirs, so who cares? On its own, it's just a word. We are creatures. And it's okay 'til we color it in. That's the fate of words and facts, and their meaning. They are coloring books whose crayons are a box of emotional ideas. And deep down, we're all in first grade.

Take, for instance, the cat we'd named TeaBag, though we didn't call her that to her face. This decisive creature's crayons were limited to primary colors. Greatly in touch with her feelings, and a total failure at controlling them. A first class conspiracy freak, unconvinced at the prospect of innocence. Us aside, everyone else was a Nazi spy to her Anne Frank. That is everyone but the "phenoms". Six or so SPECIAL people. THOSE above question. For this select few, only her obnoxious adoration would do. Reasons went unfound for these rare "Elvis" sightings. No affinity defined her hot and holy few. "Uhnh...Keep it away! O.K.? I hate cats!" Didn't matter. Even a cat lover, after a moment of vanity, might ask shouldn't she be fed, and leave rethinking the guinea pig, or anything in a cage.

Not being wishy-washy, or even remotely aware of the concept, she'd ditch the dignity and l-o-v-e bombard her helpless deity like a convicted nympho fresh outta "solitary". Down came the hair, off went the glasses, muttering a drunken, gutteral "whatever baby". Suddenly, No! meant Yesss!!

Well. Good luck if you happened to be in this Dalai Lama category of hers. Either leave the premises or submit to her scary, hairy, quasi-sex worship. Those were your options. Trying to pull her away was to pick up oiled ballbearings with your fingertips (you can't). Four years could go by since your last visit, but it was YOU! as if you'd never parted. Her Barry White platter would drop and she'd pick up right where she'd left off. No! .....vs. Aww..... Oooh baby!

Everyone else were thems of evil intention. Some needed constant surveillance from a distance that gauged your evil level, but most were just chronic nobodies, guilty but harmless, so only distant disdain was needed. This high and mighty shit can piss people off. But they didn't realize what the alternative was. You couldn't tell them, "She is really *crazy* about a few people." It only fueled the insult. She just didn't think things through, or think she needed to. You had an opinion? So what. Though it was clearly her problem, clearer was how she was gonna play it. Her way.

And why not? It was her life. And stripped of the "pet" crap she set a damn good example (conspiracies aside). The sociopathic paranoia didn't stop her from being a good creature up close. Just made her more worthy of respect, eye rolls and awe. Even if only to us.

Yeah, OKAY! I know...I know...people and their animals. People's egos and sloppy hearts. So? Somehow you've managed to not, oh...love...another...creature? Well, bravo, and what species are you? Keep it up and go unopened. Oh shit...there's my anger. Sorry. I've earned my sky miles of others' wrath. We dreamers see more than pie up there. (What's with the pie thing?)

Like I said, high and mighty shit can piss people off.

a good death

So anyway, beneath TeaBag's outer disorder, there was an endlessness of more creature to know. She, as family, was easy love. Loyal, direct, and ultimately selfless. Schizoid raptures never got directed inside our clan. She was smart and intuitive (which was good since we couldn't actually talk), and was equal in concern for the common good of the house that was the three of us. Each of us was secretly sure of being the one in charge. But faced with Chris's crumbling, she led and died first, six months before Chris.

This nice vet was her last Nazi spy, last "evil-doer". (What politic genius thumbed up on that gothic doozie? How 'bout "Trial by

Ordeal" Karl?) When nice vet felt her up, some weeks before giving her lethal injection (maybe she *was* right after all!), he'd told me it was bone cancer and helped my hands feel it in her hind leg and hip. He said that she was likely blind, that she wouldn't show she was in pain, and that "putting her down" was the thing to do. Then (in the nicest way, really), "We could do that today if you'd like." Huh? I said no, not today, and we left. I began five weeks of trying not to assess her life, but more intuit her wish, this having been our communication anyways. Well, I couldn't ask her, "Hey, today a day you might, say, wanna kick it?" now could I?

What'd always been her, normal and happy, circling on the bed, purring loud as a mountain lion ... just continued. Before when she'd been sick, like the time she managed to swallow whole an aluminum linguine off the Christmas tree, she'd hide all day'n night. Never purred or came out until an x-ray confirmed major stool softening must be employed. Then, feeling better, she reemerged. I'd cut away the trail of unshiny tinsel that dragged behind, dangling out her butt during its endless exit. (You can't just pull it out, fool!) But now she wasn't hiding. Albeit getting up on the bed was a chore, but once up, terminal diagnosis didn't seem to affect her purring with projection. Yeah, she circled me in limps, but with the same intense fervor. It just didn't say, "Kill me." But...she bumped into walls 'n stuff, didn't eat, got skinny.

People around began to suggest this "prolonging" might be cruel. I was afraid of that "cruel" possibility. Feeling I was the operative one left of us three, trying to tune in for her opinion was not so easy now, as she was chronically affectionate. Did her sad limping into things, thinness, and the stare of thick filmy eyes distress me into a point of view more others' than hers? With an "animal" we "care then spare" as a rule. Unless you're meant for eating.

And then, no less, Chris, months away from his own death, who had as much a say in the matter as I, announced it was time for "The Baby's dirt nap". Were these his self-projections? Or his insights? I was in over my head. I've blocked out what exactly prompted my cave-in, my call to the vet booking a time for the euthanasic event. I do know it wasn't clear for me then, or now. And in retrospect, it was unnatural. I feel conventions blinded me to what was, for me, a major act. So I have regrets. I wish I knew then what I...

I held her, and held her down, and felt she knew what was going on, unlikely as that might seem. And though unwanted, I felt she allowed it. She howled at the first shot. Loud, long and continually into quieter repetitions, fading noises of No! The second injection brought her to stillness. I loathe this memory because she could've had something else, not as traumatic. If I knew more then, I could have seen to it. They kindly left me alone with "her" a while. I could see that she wasn't in there anymore. I went out the door crying, clutching the empty bag, into a waiting room of people with their occupied carriers. I squeaked, "Thanks you guys, sniff...if I ever get another cat...gnk...I'll be back." I oughta rent myself out.

Sitting in the car afterwards, the awful truth was that it may have been a day or at all...too soon. In my view, I interrupted her.

And it's no convenience now. It wasn't good.

There's no crayon for this.

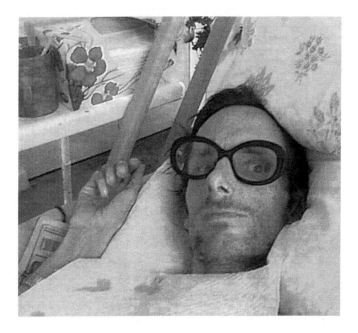

Easter Sunday

April 4th, 1999

He was still here, in what'd become the cruel stranger, the one-time him, his "me" gone, a bony stretch of skin holding him here. Spared now, his wide eyes stared out alert and un-lidded into a private intensity. This melted the unnecessary me. The worn out caregiver was suddenly useless. Quicker than you can rudely say "see-ya", it vamoosed and I was admitted in. Into the stunning scene of him. Only now allowed to me in its full weight...because, it was natural. He was here, just not the part of him that was vulnerable. He was, today, safe as a persona of awesome focus, far above what one could have imagined. And he was never more himself, never more alive. And *he* had been a creature of focus.

a good death

I petted and stroked an available spot, and spoke without intending or expecting to wake him. With his eyes so open, it seemed impossible that light wasn't entering. I wondered how long he would stay in this state, but wondered without imagining him reentering to awful realities or exiting the unknown. That clean kind of thought was a wonderful gift. There were no mental excursions to what answers would bring, i.e. a long coma would mean further decomposition, or worse he would reawaken to experience the more of it. Or he would die. No, I just wondered completely without thought of answer. I was in a trusting place. I won't call it a fog because everything felt so clear. I s'pose the protective policeman in me had gathered all its cumbersome gear and neurotic dedication...and left. Leaving room for my heart.

It was as if he was sharing an aspect of where he was with me. He was helping me.

At 11am, Sonya, the home care aid on Sunday, came. I told her I had to go to the restaurant to install some light fixtures. Wiring required turning fuses off, so it had to be done before noon when they opened. As if some dumb brunch should matter at this point in life. I had been trained like Pavlov's dogs. But I was my own worst whip. Apparently, all of me wasn't ready.

Sonya tried not to, but she looked scared. How sweet she was in that moment. I told her I'd be back soon and told her to call me on my cell phone if she needed anything. I drove downtown, parked, and did the work. Not being an electrician, I didn't finish 'til 12:30... In the car on my way back uptown my phone rang. It was Sonya. She told me that the IV drip computer was beeping, indicating the morphine bag would soon be empty. The increase in dose went through the morphine bag quicker. I'd have thought of this before I'd left, but I was without the usual innate "militia". She said that our friend, Sandy Bell, had come by and was there, and that Chris's breathing was different. I said I'd be right there, hung up, and calmly broke a few traffic laws. I didn't wonder anything.

I came into the apartment, saw his distinct change into shallow breathing, his eyes still wide open, and I knew it was approaching. After I addressed the drug bag, I thanked Sonya and told her it would be better if she went home. She left bluely as Sandy went in to say goodbye. Sandy came out visibly upset. I hugged her and said I was going in and closing the door. How difficult for her to stay alone, out on the couch, with her imaginings to keep her company. What generosity inspired her? Especially given her self-professed difficult relation with death. Her father was "stolen" in a road accident when she was eleven. I don't recall asking her to leave or stay. Yet she stayed.

I got in the bed behind Chris, who was on his side, and "made spoons". Something we hadn't done in ages given the bedsore and pain it would have caused. His presence felt confident, not comatose. I'd forgotten how when we'd be going somewhere he'd get on me about getting out the door. Now, after years of natural role confusion, he was driving again.

My face was lightly resting on the back of his bony head so as to speak in his ear. My arms twined around on top and above him, holding and stroking. I know my face was all wet and snotty. I knew my heart was breaking, but it didn't hurt. As if by osmosis, he was sharing his morphine. I talked about TeaBag waiting, about how his grandmother would be coming along soon. I asked him to leave part of himself in the small of my back for as long he could. It occurred to me that I might be being physically obnoxious at such a time and said as much, laughing, not to myself. It could have only been funny in the context of our shared sense of humor.

Easter Sunday

It occurred to me to call his parents. I reached for the phone and dialed his mom. She wasn't home, but en route from Long Island. So, it was the answering machine. Regretfully, I left a message trying to convey his peaceful state. I called his dad and wife Martha. They both got on the phone. I held it to his ear so they each could speak. In the case of his dad, I felt, as I held the phone, that it seemed cruel. But I also felt it would have been wrong to not make of the opportunity. He is like Chris in so many ways. He may berate himself for not being easy with words. But I'd disagree. I have so much respect for him. I didn't hear what was said, so I wasn't sure how long to hold the phone to his ear. Hoping not to interrupt, I eventually put it to mine and said hi. We expressed love, and I said I'd call later. I had to go now.

I told Chris that if it hurt ... blink ... and I'd give him a bolus. I didn't know if he even could blink. At another point I said that if I was crowding him...blink. I didn't question if he could hear. About ten or fifteen minutes later he made a very slow .... deliberate ..... blink. I pushed the bolus button. I began laughing, saying how I didn't give any options. Like maybe two blinks would mean no bolus, or that maybe the blink meant stop snotting in my ear and get fucking off of me. I'm trying to fucking die here. Well, OK, it was the best I could do, and yes, he was stuck with it. I'm not sorry.

We were where we could best be. Where we'd always tried to be. We struggle anyway, might as well optimize. He was, as unalone as possible, as he had probably felt in a long, long time. And I had come as far as is allowed. Through all the veils of each of one's own "whatevers" it takes to stay. To come to the surface long enough to see a goal, and inquire beyond hazy answers, so as to find and make concrete arrangements, assert desires, not for ego or defiance, but just.... to know that in this of all moments, there's security. An uninterruptable place to leap out from. Into what we can't know from here. An unavoided nowhere.

Then a gift for me, initially physical then mental image ... neither mine. Something electric spiraled up and out through me. It seemed to start small in my upper legs and moved up, widening till it exited out my top. It was accompanied by an involuntary curve on my mouth, not mine, a smirky twitch the shape of Chris's Jughead side smile. In the final instance of this electric swirl came the image of him running joyfully around and out, as this current. Full bodied. It formed an able and ageless Chris. An unpent energy galloping out the top of my head, leaving his smile on my face. For some reason it made me twist my head around to look at the clock. 5:24pm. I turned my head back to resume my previously unbroken vigil, and for a moment, then two..... three.......Four..... There were no more intakes of air. Ever.

So after what seemed an eternity, he ran happily, free from judgment, internal or external. And he made it so as to run through me. Not away, but with certainty toward and into things I can't know of or see. This is the gift he could leave for me. Moreover I could feel his stretching back the rules in a characteristic bratty noncompliance, just to offer it. I know the electric rotary was for my benefit. Fits of rage and love.

I don't wonder about it. Our connection is larger than any reassurance unforthcoming. His life is larger than us. He goes on, and I don't wonder or worry where or how. Wish I could share why I know this, but I can't. I can only assure you that I do. And hope that reflecting glimpses of how I got here might help you.

I had pinned up lots of pictures on the wall opposite the foot of his bed. TeaBag, the nuba, friends, things to keep his remaining earthliness possibly engaged. And some vines of silk flowers from the 99 cent store. I felt an unforeseen glow of achievement. I'd the honor of giving birth......to his greatest achievement.

The room had power. As a bare stage's moment of triumph, after a show sits electric in the silence, when a stunned audience's heart collectively moves in a wave of the all of it. Including the end. And on that wall, there were three butterflies, framed under glass...And though they no longer took earthly flights......Butterflies, were and are, still in attendance...

AFTERWORD

Chris died peacefully in my arms at home in the Aurora 12C-1. I wrapped myself around him and chewed on his ear and got a lot of snot in his hair and talked steadily of the past, the present, and the future. He was so ready and helped me to be also.

Soon after, I was surrounded by friends. Grant cooked pasta. Alan phoned his way through the arrangements. Sandra sobbed and choked in the bathroom. Bill and Joan came up the elevator with the Reddens Funeral guys. Chris's mom came over with her boyfriend. Her face looked like a big bruised apple, and of course, my heart went out to her.

I wanted nothing to do with memorial gatherings. The funeral home took his body away strapped upright on a hand truck. I cannot tolerate the memory. I wanted no more.

Chris said he wanted his ashes to go in the Chesapeake Bay. Sometime in the last months he had a conversation with Alan in which a tree planting was discussed. He told me he wanted some of his ashes to go in a magnolia at Grant and Alan's house. The bay became his father's, and the tree became his mother's by default. There isn't a word that describes my apprehension of attending.

The Tuesday prior to the first anniversary of Chris's death, his mom called and pointedly asked when the planting would be. I said I was sorry but I couldn't preside, arrange, or take part in contemplating it. Just plant the tree. She called Alan, and they decided on that Sunday, as Chris's mom was concerned that it should happen as soon as possible. They understood that I might or might not come. On Saturday, I decided to go. Alone. I never called to inform or invite people. I never decided not to inform or invite people.

The tree is beautiful. Grant and Alan did such a nice job. I say it because they did. What I don't say in truth is that I barely looked after I saw the ashes, except to take two or three side-glances at figures on a hill doing something I can't bear the thought of. No one was there. It made me blind. I felt only guilt for them having to take over. It was that way before I went – and after. I didn't want to say later, 'if only I had done it differently', so I tried to follow my instincts, but they didn't come.

For me there is no closure. I couldn't begin to share my grief, or pretend to do so at that time. This doesn't mean I stopped living or that I minimized or didn't appreciate others' feelings of loss.

One by one I have experienced disapproval and anger from each of my friends on this, and it is so agonizing. My mind wonders what on earth does each of them think I am doing? Don't any of them realize? I have been faced with awesome challenges.

I am afraid of being judged.

I am afraid of not being tolerated.

Christopher Clements, 1961-1999

John Noonan, 1956-2007

Made in the USA
Middletown, DE
08 October 2015